Honey Bees

I0145851

Victoria Blakemore

© 2017 Victoria Blakemore

All rights reserved. This book or parts thereof may not be reproduced in any form, stored in any retrieval system, or transmitted in any form by any means—electronic, mechanical, photocopy, recording, or otherwise—without prior written permission of the publisher, except as provided by United States of America copyright law. For permission requests, write to the publisher, at "Attention: Permissions Coordinator," at the address below.

vblakemore.author@gmail.com

Copyright info/picture credits

Cover, Maciej Olszewski/AdobeStock; Page 3, MargyS/Pixabay; Page 5, philpace/Pixabay; Page 7, philpace/Pixabay; Page 9, Kanenori/Pixabay; Pages 10-11, tpsdave/Pixabay; Page 13, Oldiefan/Pixabay; Page 15, abidbh6/Pixabay; Page 17, Oldiefan/Pixabay; Page 19, sumikophoto/AdobeStock; Page 21, kostik2photo/AdobeStock; Page 23; Roman Pyshchyk/AdobeStock; Page 25, Maciej Olszewski/AdobeStock; Page 27, catkin/Pixabay; Page 29, Pexels/Pixabay; Page 31, Daria-Yakovleva/Pixabay; Page 33, tpsdave/Pixabay; Page 35, bernswaelz/Pixabay

Table of Contents

What are Honey Bees?   2

Kinds of Honey Bees   4

Physical Characteristics   6

Habitat   8

Range   10

Collecting Pollen   12

Diet   14

Communication   16

Movement   18

Hive Life   20

Life Cycle   22

Bee Jobs   24

Self Defense   26

Beekeepers   28

Honey   30

Population   32

Helping Bees   34

Glossary   36

What Are Honey Bees?

Honey bees are small insects that are known for their black and yellow stripes.

Like other insects, they have six legs and a **segmented** body.

Honey bees have fine hairs all over their body.

Kinds of Honey Bees

There are six main kinds of honey bees.

They differ in their color, how much honey they produce, where they live, and how **aggressive** they are.

Most honey bees are black
and yellow, but they can
also be gray, brown, and
black.

Physical Characteristics

Honey bees have antennae

that help them to sense

flowers.

They also have pollen

baskets on two of their legs.

They are special pouches

that honey bees use to store

pollen that they collect.

Honey bee eyes allow them
to see very fast motion. They
can see things that human
eyes can't.

Habitat

Honey bees are found in many different habitats. They need places with lots of flowering plants.

Honey bees are often seen in forests, meadows, orchards, and gardens.

Range

Honey bees are found on every continent except Antarctica.

Honey bees that live in colder places have to work hard to keep the hive warm in winter.

Collecting Pollen

Bees collect pollen and nectar from flowers. The hair on their bodies collects the pollen.

They use their tube-shaped tongues to suck nectar out of flowers and bring it back to the hive.

Diet

Bees store the nectar that they get from flowers in the hive.

They use their wings to flap air onto the nectar to help it form into honey. The honey is stored to be used as food.

Nectar and honey are stored in waxy cells that are called **honeycombs.**

Communication

Honey bees have a special dance that tells other honey bees where they have found nectar.

The dances are used to tell how far away the nectar is and which direction it is in.

They also have dances that

tell other honey bees if they

need help collecting nectar

or making honey. **17**

Movement

Honey bees have very small wings for an insect of their size.

They flap their wings about 230 times per second when they are in flight. They have been known to fly as fast as twenty miles per hour.

Honey bees that are
carrying pollen and nectar
are not as fast because of
the extra weight.

Hive Life

Bees are social insects and live in a large group, which is called a colony. The colony's home is a hive.

In the wild, hives are usually found in hollow trees or between rocks.

Life Cycle

Bee eggs are laid by the queen bee. The eggs hatch into larva.

Larva are taken care of by worker bees until they are big enough to form a pupa.

After they form a pupa, they
will finish their life cycle by
growing into an adult bee.

Bee Jobs

There are three kinds of bees in the hive. The queen bee lays the eggs.

Drones are male bees that live in the hive. They help the queen.

24

Worker bees collect pollen and nectar, build the hive, and protect the hive from predators.

Self Defense

Honey bees have a sharp stinger that they can use as a defense. Honey bees that are left alone do not usually sting.

When you are stung, **venom** is pumped into the **wound** until the stinger is removed.

Bees die after they sting

something, so they are unlikely

to sting you unless you bother

them.

27

Beekeepers

Beekeepers are people who have hives of bees that they take care of. They **harvest** the honey, honeycomb, and beeswax from their hives.

Some farmers set up hives on their farms so their crops are **pollinated**.

Beekeepers wear special clothing to keep them safe from bee stings when they are working with the hives.

29

Honey

Honey has several health benefits. It can soothe a sore throat and help if you have a cough. It can also help your heart to stay healthy.

Eating local honey can help people with allergies because it contains local pollen.

Population

Honey bee populations have been getting smaller. Some threats that face honey bees are **pesticides**, disease, and habitat loss.

The vorroa destructor mite is a **parasite** that can live in a hive and kill honey bees.

Without honey bees, many foods that we eat would no longer be **plentiful**.

Helping Bees

There are many ways that people are trying to help honey bees.

People can plant flowers that bees like to provide them with pollen. They can also stay away from using pesticides.

Some people build beehives in
their gardens so that bee colonies
have a safe place to live.

Glossary

Aggressive: likely to attack

Harvest: gathering ripe crops

Honeycomb: a group of cells in a hive where bees store honey

Parasite: a plant or animal that feeds on the energy of another animal

Pesticides: chemicals that are used to kill insects on crops

Plentiful: more than enough

Pollinated: when pollen is moved from one plant to another, allowing crops to grow

Segmented: split into separate parts

Venom: a poison that some animals make

Wound: an injury

About the Author

Victoria Blakemore is a first grade

teacher in Southwest Florida with a

passion for reading.

You can visit her at

www.elementaryexplorers.com

Also in This Series

Gray Wolves	Sloths	Flamingos	Camels	Koalas	Honey Bees	Pandas
Pangolins	White-Tailed Deer	Orcas	Giraffes	Corn	Meerkats	Echidnas
Walruses	Raccoons	Bald Eagles	Apples	Arctic Foxes	Red Pandas	Cassowaries
Tigers	Ladybugs	Moose	Beluga Whales	Leopards	Elephants	Jellyfish
Binturongs	Lions	Dolphins	Reindeer	Hammerhead Sharks	Hippos	Pumpkins
Peafowl	Chameleons	Florida Panthers	Aye-Ayes	Black Bears	Cheetahs	Manatees
Gingerbread	Polar Bears	Hot Chocolate	Orangutans	Coyotes	Marshmallows	Strawberries

Victoria Blakemore

Also in This Series

Aardvarks	Mako Sharks	Alligators	Frogs	Hedgehogs	Brown Bears	Bongos
Sea Turtles	Quokkas	Muskrats	Zebras	Red Foxes	Ring-Tailed Lemurs	Platypuses
Anteaters	Kangaroos	Rhinos	Jaguars	Wombats	Capybaras	Gorillas
Cats	Skunks	Butterflies	Dingoes	Snow Leopards	African Wild Dogs	Penguins
Whale Sharks	Wolverines	Warthogs	Caracals	Badgers	Seals	Hummingbirds
Pikas	Humpback Whales	Pumas	Lemonade	Llamas	Tulips	Ostriches
Sunflowers	Fennec Foxes	Sea Lions	Squirrels	Roses	Porcupines	Ice Cream

Each cover reads: Elementary Explorers — Victoria Blakemore

www.ingramcontent.com/pod-product-compliance
Lightning Source LLC
Chambersburg PA
CBHW041218030426
42336CB00023B/3386